ISBN 9798655929920

CHAPTER 1: NEW YORK

"I want to live in New Zealand," I told my mum. Years later, when my friend Rita moved to Christchurch, I was rather put off by stories of restaurants that shut at 5 pm. No thanks, that's not for me.

In the 1950s, upon leaving school, lots of young girls took a shorthand and typing course. You could aim to be the boss's secretary. I didn't want to do that; it would pigeon hole me in one place.

I wanted to travel. Then people mainly only knew what they read about. Television rarely showed anything international, and most people didn't even have a set. To learn and see things you had to visit.

My first long trip was many years before I joined Pan Am. It was a coach tour as lots of people did back then. On the return, I caught my first flight. It was in a converted freighter, with canvas, perhaps netting for seats. It was deafening, and it made me feel sick. After twenty minutes I swore I'd never get on a plane again.

That's where my journey really begins when I thought it had ended.

MaxFactor gave me a chance to travel. I made some beautiful friends, but travelling around the country living in hotels grows lonely. So I moved to work for Otis, sharing a house with my old MaxFactor friends.

Eight years after that first flight, I was sitting on a train going home, and I actually got a seat. A rare treat. I'd bought a paper as I always did, I wasn't really looking for a job, but it was still interesting to look at the adverts. One advert was for an airline, "Pan American". Everyone had heard of them, but I knew nothing about their jobs.

When I got home, I chatted to the girls I shared with, and they told me to give it a go. The most surprising thing was to actually get a reply to my application!

I was interviewed and told the job was mine. That staggered me, I didn't really know anything about the job at all. However, the pay was good and being able to travel sounded nice. So I said yes. Mr Island interviewed me, a very nice man, he was the manager there for quite a long time. He asked me about different countries, and if I knew where they were. Fortunately, as I've always been interested in other countries, I was able to answer his questions, OK.

When I started, only two weeks later, I did a course. I learned about places I'd never heard of before, and how to check up on them. I got a commendation. Why? Well, I looked at the index to find the answers; apparently, that's a good thing. Pan Am had a training room, run by Mrs Ruth Hole. She was in her late fifties, helpful, never raised her voice and really encouraging. She had been there for many years. The training room was right next door to reservations. They had modern computers.

That meant they had a daisy wheel, rather like typewriters, but no screens at all. They were linked by an early form of the internet, to New York. A large cable travelled under the sea, and they'd quite regularly be ripped up accidentally by fishermen.

After the course, all four of us were told we'd passed. Then, on Friday afternoon, they asked if our passports were up to date. We were all told, "you're going to New York on Monday". We were being sent to New York to learn about our computer system, plus to see just how big Pan Am really was. Pan American, as it was back then, was a name we all had heard of, but not a company we knew much about or appreciated the size of.

My mum and dad couldn't believe it. But as everything was arranged, and I had been travelling all over with my previous job, they rather accepted it. My flatmate Gerry, who lives in Canada now, said she too might try to get a job with the airlines. She had been a dancer who had danced with the Bluebells in Paris. So she liked the idea. Eventually, she got a job with UTA, who were a French airline.

Going to New York was exciting. I'd never been through customs and immigration before. It was a DC8 jet, I remember that because DC8's had their controls in the seat in front, but on 707's you had to reach up over your head. Ruth Hole had stressed the importance of doing leg and foot exercises. To this day, I still do them when I travel aboard a coach or a train.

When we landed, we had to queue for ages. However, the people were very friendly. Pan Am always tried to get you through ahead of an Alitalia flight, because their passengers always carried food. You were not allowed to take any food into America. Unfortunately, on that occasion, we ended up behind them. Oh well. Then we were picked up by a limousine, something rare outside of America at that time.

Until we hit Manhattan, it was not very inspiring. Arriving we all dumped our cases, you had to carry cases then, no wheels like now. Having come about lunchtime, my first impression of Manhattan was the height of all buildings. You looked down the street, and they all went up so high. They just went up, all of them, not just some, all of them. That was my first impression of New York. You don't notice that today, because of the crowds. Back in the 1960s pavements weren't as packed, so you could see.

We got a meal in a cafe in the hotel. It was the height of Beatle mania, every second question was about the Beatles, they'd flown there on Pan Am. I remember Johnny Carson interviewing Sammy Davis Jnr. He said, "don't ask me about the Beatles, not even I can get tickets, and my children don't believe me!".

The training was good, I enjoyed it. One of the staff took us to where they went shopping. Although Macy's was the biggest store in the world, at a nearby basement shop, you could get Macy's clothes much cheaper. We bought some bits, but shopping wasn't really on our minds.

I loved the breakfasts in New York. All the different ways they'd do your eggs! For lunch, I remember my first caesar salad in the staff canteen. It was the first time I'd seen all the different foods in cabinets, back then that was very modern. Little things like that were new and fascinating.

We went up to the 44th floor. There was a special lift which didn't stop anywhere else. The whole level had armed guards to protect the computers. It was quite astounding.

The Pan Am Building is fantastic. You don't quite grasp the enormous size. How dare they change the name on it! It was nice, and there was a pleasant atmosphere.

I think we stayed at the Lexington Hotel, but it was only for four days, plus travel time.

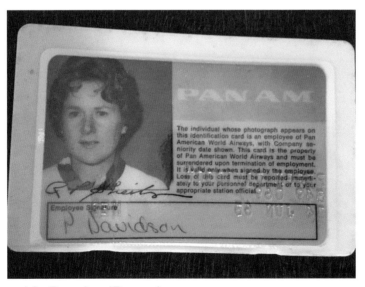

My Pan Am ID card

CHAPTER 2: RIO WITH MY SISTER

Finding myself now able to, I booked a short trip for my mum and dad. That had sort of been a success, but not in all ways.

I then thought about my sister Ann. My brothers were either married or too young. So I booked it for Ann and me, plus my friend Maureen.

I remember meeting Ann and some of her friends at the railway station. From there we went out to the airport.

We had to stop overnight in New York. Maureen said she'd stayed in the YWCA and it was perfectly fine. I was very nervous, having brought Ann there because New York wasn't a safe place. I didn't want anything to happen to my sister.

The YWCA wasn't perfectly fine, it was horrendous. It was riddled with cockroaches. Thankfully we arrived in the evening and left in the morning. I was happy to check out.

I seem to remember we then caught Avianca to Brazil. It was a good flight. The plane stopped in Brazillia, which was Brazil's capital. Just before landing, we flew in a giant circle looking down on fabulously modern and unique buildings. It would have been fascinating to explore them. I imagine that it isn't quite so advanced looking now.

In Rio, we stayed at the Gloria Hotel. It was an older hotel, but a beautiful place. I didn't want to take my sister Ann to a grotty hotel!

I recall breakfast was included, but you couldn't get a good cup of coffee. All of the good coffee was exported! That was no good for Ann or me as we both like a coffee.

Still, throughout the day, we found beautiful hot beef sandwiches. Although there were tourists, we were a bit of a novelty. So they'd usually put a little bit of extra meat in our sandwiches.

Copacabana Beach was very beautiful, very sandy. It was full of boys playing football. Unfortunately for some reason, my legs came up in blisters. I'd never had that before or since, but we did mean we had to leave. We did, however, also make it to Ipanema Beach.

We used local buses to get about, which was quite brave in those days. That was something we enjoyed. Brazilian people were courteous and friendly.

We went up to the statue of Christ the Redeemer. Far less touristy were the many local markets, and we enjoyed those.

We got invited to a big football match by a marching band who were playing at the interval. Being me, I'd have gone. However, Maureen bluntly told them we already had plans. I thought it was a shame, going to a football match in Brazil would have been fantastic.

Power cuts were reasonably frequent. On one occasion I'd nipped out, and Maureen walked up the emergency stairs in pitch black to check Ann wasn't stuck in a lift. I've no idea why she would have been, but it was a lovely thing to do.

I remember Ann and I chatting that seeing Rio in the future on the television would be exciting, because we'd be able to say, "I was there!". We've often mentioned to each other when one of us has seen somewhere from that trip.

That was my only trip to South America!

CHAPTER 3: INDIA

India is a long way to go for just four days! We flew out on Air India, at least they are still going!

We were somewhat surprised to be told that our hotel would be completely locked for the first day. There was a festival where paint is thrown over everyone. Our hotel refused to let them on their grounds. So our first day in New Delhi was spent watching from afar.

The next day we went into a temple, leaving our shoes at the door. We didn't expect them to still be there upon our return, but luckily they were.

We were taken to a fortress, where all the stonework was red. Beyond that, we wandered around, fighting off beggars.

We went about it in the wrong way, by giving them money. All they did was simply to get their friends, they knew a soft touch. It was heartbreaking, and we all felt we had to do something. The money we gave them was pence, but it was a lot to them.

It was rumoured that children were deliberately disfigured so they could go begging. I have no idea if that is true. It seemed odd that there were so many disabled children, but with basically no healthcare, who knows what complications might happen.

Back at the hotel, there was a card for someone who would make clothes. So I had a go, ordering some of their trousers. We were in hysterics when they came the next day, they were like giant clown trousers on me. So much for their measuring up!

You could eat either Western or Indian food. The building was in an old colonial style, with a man pulling a giant cord to turn a ceiling fan. I was the only one silly enough to order Indian, and I paid the price.

New Delhi looked very colonial, with cows wandering freely. All the women wore saris. We were shown how to wear a sari, but it never looked as good on us.

On the third day, we were taken out to the Taj Mahal. Going out early in the morning, you saw women coming back from the rivers, with massive jugs balanced on their head. It looked like something out of the bible.

At the Taj Mahal, we stayed at Clark's Hotel. By the gate, there was a man with a basket and a pipe. As we came out, he started to play and out of his basket, a cobra popped up. Needless to say, we didn't get too close.

That evening we went to the Taj Mahal. The Taj Mahal is built, so the sides are identical. There is a time during each month when the light is precisely over the halfway point. That happened to be that when we visited. So we just sat and watched, it was stunning.

Many years later, Princess Diana would follow us, and have her most iconic photograph taken exactly where I sat.

Heading back to New Delhi, we had a few hours left before our flight. So our chauffeur nipped out to get some bottles of coke. A little boy, maybe six or seven, was there. He ran off, my friend John Rankmore joked that I'd done something to scare him. It turned out they'd seen my friend Marion, who had lace-up shoes on. Everybody else had sandals. He came back with his friends, and none of them could believe it. Nobody had shoes in this part of India, just sandals. I'm sure they thought she had strange feet.

CHAPTER 4: PHILADELPHIA & THE AMISH

One of the first trips as a representative of Pan Am was to Philadelphia. We were guests of the mayor. We'd been invited because the mayor wanted passengers to book Philadelphia for Washington. We got invited up to his office. The mayor gave us a talk about the area and encouraged us to offer Philadelphia as a stopover. He was very welcoming and approachable, he seemed like a nice guy. I don't know what one expects a mayors office to be like, but it was quite ordinary apart from the flags. From Philadelphia, there was a speedy train service to Baltimore, Washington or New York.

Philadelphia was clearly a more suburban town than New York. Philadelphia had a lot more fresh vegetables than New York. At that time, American food always looked great, and there was masses of it. However, it's taste never quite lived up to the looks. So I tended to go for a salad.

Philadelphian people were really friendly, they wanted to know where you were from and were very welcoming. They were very proud of their London bus. At that time, it was the only double-decker tour bus in America.

We were given a small model of the liberty bell to take back, complete with crack. Of course, the first American Flag was also made in Philadelphia by Betsy Ross. There is a lot of history associated with the city.

The big attraction was the Amish People. They were incredible, and visiting was like stepping back in time. Ladies wore black skirts and bonnets, men had long beards, long black coats and black trilby type hats. There were a few brick houses, but mostly they lived in farm style properties, with gas lamps. They had no cars, no electricity and went everywhere by horse and buggy. The Amish are well known for their horse breeding. They mostly worked on the land, but a few people worked in shops selling crafts. I bought a bonnet, but never ever wore it.

They were pleasant but kept themselves to themself. If you spoke politely, the Amish would answer, and I think it helped that we were from far away. They realised their community was a curiosity but were open to visitors. They could be quite harsh if someone left the community, though.

AWAY FROM HOME—These Londoners came all the way to the countryside outside of Philadelphia, Pennsylvania, to see—a London bus. The double-decker is used by the Downingtown Inn resort to carry its guests to and from the airport and for local sightseeing. Allen Harper (second from left), sales director of the Inn, points out its features to LON staffers Dave Blott, Don McCulloch, Peggy Davidson, Peter Burrage and Ray Evans.

From Philadelphia (left) my picture in Pan Am's Clipper Newspaper (below) official photograph I'm rear second left

CHAPTER 5: ACCOMPANYING MINORS

Speaking of Philadelphia, something I was asked to do on several occasions, was accompanying school children. That involved taking the child on the flight, making sure they were met by the right person, before turning around and flying back.

My next time back in Philadelphia was escorting a child. On that occasion, I stayed overnight, but I was too early to check-in. So I asked at the cloakroom if they could please store my coat, "oh no, we can't touch fur madam", he responded. Deadpan, I replied, "it's not real". He couldn't believe it!

The first child I accompanied was a little girl travelling to Boston. Her family were lovely. There was no question who her parents were because she flew at them upon arrival! The girl liked stories, so I read a lot to her. The mother thanked me and said the girl had a lovely time. They took me back to their house, offered me lunch and a lie down before I headed back that night. I was almost sorry to leave them! Her family name frequently comes up associated with movies and television, so I often wonder if there is a link.

I never really quizzed the children. Mary McDonald, a supervisor I was friendly with, had said not to. You never know what the children might say. I might have asked had she not tipped me off. Mary told me to act like a teacher and read to them. Back then there was no in-flight entertainment, but most of the children had some favourite books with them.

I'm not sure why I did it or was asked. Maybe I seemed trustworthy? I seem to remember they gave me some extra days off, but it wasn't paid.

On another occasion, I took a small boy to Hong Kong. I almost got offloaded halfway. The boy was fine and sleepy, I suspect he'd been given something, not by me! Halfway they'd overbooked the flight, I forget where exactly. So I was told as staff I'd have to get off. When I explained about the minor, the purser said, "oh no, you're not getting off anywhere, we haven't got the time to keep an eye on him." She fetched the captain who decided, "no way can you get off, there's no one to look after him." So I managed to avoid being offloaded, even if we both ended up getting somewhat wet from a leaking toilet. His family invited me to stop and stay when we arrived, but I was continuing to the Philippines.

CHAPTER 6: STAYING ON BASE, VISITING MY USAF FRIENDS

I also spent a lot of time with a girl from Liverpool, who was married to an American. He was, in fact, a Mormon from near Salt Lake City. He was a lovely man who put no pressure on Terry to convert. She would have done, but they are not allowed to drink caffeinated tea, which is not a proper cup of tea for a lady from Liverpool.

The first time I stayed with them was in the Philippines for a month. I met them in Manila, but their base was further north.

Clark Airforce Base was a big place, and all the houses were physically on base, something that is not always the case. They had a Filipino maid, which they warned me about in the car. Neither knew how to treat a maid, and little things niggled them. Merrill hated it because it was like having a stranger in the house. Part of the agreement between the US and Filipino Government was that every family employed a local maid.

I thought she was nice. Perhaps having a third person about in the day helped. She made beautiful crochet tops, and it must have been hard for her to live away from home. Terry and I shopped off base a lot because everything was so cheap.

Artists would paint your photo for you. I did' t buy anything because it would have been a pain on the aircraft. However the US Air Force had a generous shipping allowance, so Terry bought up furniture and all sorts.

I bought a beautiful ornament, which I still have in the living room.

We got a bus to Baguio, which is right up north in the Philippines. The men there wear something very similar to kilts. I understand it is a national costume, but it was a surprise to see people actually wearing it. Travelling by bus, wow. It was the kind of trip you see on television, but never imagine taking. Several people had baskets with chickens in them.

We didn't have long in Baguio. It was clear that people were very different there. They were country people. They were lovely people, so friendly and very impressed that we caught a bus with them.

We went to the market. The ladies were going through their hair. Terry asked me if I knew what they were doing? I said no, she told me they were picking nits out of each other's hair.

We also used to go out with a group of wives from the base. For them, the big thing was shopping, because everything was so cheap. You had to be careful because it was common for wood to have woodworm.

In the Philippines, we always had pizza when going out. Why? Because we knew what it was. At that time the US Air Force gave a lot of instructions about how to act off base. I am not sure if they still do. The Air Force was very concerned about making sure that local people were treated well. They didn't want any offence to be taken if you didn't like the food. So pizza was a diplomatically safe option!

Manila isn't a place I got to tour around. I caught a bus from Clark to Manila and then a taxi to my hotel next to the airport. There was an enormous storm, and the highway was flooded. I've got no idea how my bus got through. The buildings were tropical, ones that get blown down easily, but put back up quickly afterwards too. It was very underdeveloped.

Attached to the hotel was a village, rather like a museum. I went around it naturally, but in reality, it was lots of little shops selling shells and things made from shells. They were so inexpensive. It seemed wrong not to buy. The Philippines were doing it tough,

Imelda was busy buying shoes, and the prices were so cheap for tourists, but of course not for locals.

My next time staying with Terry and Merrill was really different. It was up in Washington State, way in the middle of nowhere. I think Merrill did something with computers. At that time, the US was developing its early warning system, and that's what I believe the base existed for. That is just my own opinion.

I flew to Seattle. Between terminal buildings was the first automatic train I'd ever been on. There was no driver, long before elsewhere - it was good, clean and very modern looking. Riding on something without a driver was quite exciting - it was the 1960s. That took me to a little local plane.

I flew that to Pasco, now called Tricity Airport. Three people got off, me and two others. The plane was in early, so I got chatting. There was only one employee at the airport. He talked the pilot in - it was pretty hilly - then he got the passengers off, followed by their luggage, before seeing the plane off. It was a lovely little airport, and the employee thought it was great. No one was looking over his shoulder, and his hours changed around the flights.

Their house was in a hamlet, a little miniature village up in the mountains, not on base. My main memory was that Terry hated it. The atmosphere on base was very political, everyone was watching what you did, with a lot of jealousy about promotions. Apart from walking there was nothing to do. Film nights were put on, but there wasn't a cinema or anything. People were friendly to me, but their whole life was the air force. I don't think a single person wanted to be there. The people weren't as social as most bases either.

There was nothing much around apart from a damn. That is where I had my first Mexican food from a street vendor along the highway. I'd go back there just to have the food! There was no talk then about them being illegals or not, the locals were welcoming with no aggro. It was an excellent place for a weekend because the area was gorgeous. Any longer and you'd be stuck for things to do.

At least the volcano didn't go off when I was there!

My next time visiting was Sacramento. At that time, I was working three days on and three days off. So, being just up the road from San Francisco, I could visit easily without taking much time off. Sacramento is the capital of California. I don't remember much about the city itself. It struck me as a generic

American city. You get used to the smaller ones being very similar.

They were not living on base then. At that time, there was quite a bit of racial prejudice everywhere. A lot of servicemen were Black American's with white wives. There were a lot of places the air force couldn't send them, but Sacramento was accepting.

I met many of the couples, including husbands and children, of course. We were invited somewhere for afternoon tea every day. They'd bring out their finest tea sets, all with beautiful teapots and lovely cakes. Some of them had been through rough times, so to meet people who were accepting was nice for them. The only problem was I don't drink tea, so I had to ask Terry to let them know! It was nice to able to do it, they'd lived through rough times and society hadn't been kind to them.

My other memory was learning how to make a paper mache pig money box. I still have it to this day. Strangely their daughter is now living at RAF Lakenheath.

When I left school, my friend Rita and I went to an International Club. There was a lot of prejudice towards people from Africa or Asia. It was interesting because the Pakistani and Indian's used to dine out together. After all, it was an opportunity they'd never get back home. So it wasn't just America where prejudice existed.

The last place I visited them was New Mexico. I fell in love with New Mexico. It was so different, with a real Spanish influence. Holloman Air Force Base was literally in the middle of nowhere. So we didn't visit many places. It was surrounded by desert. With no mobile phones, driving far was something you didn't do for safety reasons. The base had everything, with a little shopping mall, nothing fancy, but there was a lot of facilities.

Holloman was famous for housing the space monkeys. These chimps were the first creatures sent into space. However, when they put a base in the middle of nowhere, it's important. That means you don't ask questions. To get access, the guards took my passport and tickets. I also had my Pan Am ID with me, which carried a lot of weight with the US air force.

I was there for Christmas, and we went shopping on Christmas day! Seers had a big sale on. I still have the purple and white sheets I bought there to this day. Our sheets were all very muted, not colourful like Seers!

In those days one used Travellers Cheques, which in America had to be cashed at a bank. The local bank had never actually come across one before. They didn't know what rate of exchange to use, but luckily I had the rate a bank in Dallas had used. So they decided to use that rate. I was very grateful for their help. The staff were excited because they never had visitors from overseas. Months later, at home, I got a cheque in the post. The manager had confirmed the official rate later on that day. He'd discovered that I was owed a few dollars, so he posted me a cheque. I wrote back to say how grateful I was.

New Mexican's were much more Mexican than American. So the culture was very different.

A friend of Terry's spent a lot of time with us, I wish I could remember her name. The three of us went everywhere together, going over to her's or out for a coffee. We had a lovely time. She gave me a beautiful brass letter rack, which I still have in my lounge. On my last day, she cooked me breakfast, my favourite French Toast. It snowed on my way to the airport, in the desert, a fantastic co-incidence.

CHAPTER 7: LAS VEGAS

Terry and Merrill eventually moved to Las Vegas, but unfortunately, I never saw them there.

I did visit Las Vegas once though. It was an airline sponsored trip, but I can't remember which one. We were picked up at the airport. My first impression was that I expected a much bigger airport, but there were poker machines all through arrivals.

I've tried on many occasions to look up which hotel I stayed at, but I can't recall. It was massive, no queue for check-in, we just walked straight up. Not like today where it could easily be an hour's wait. The others were all up on the second floor, but I was on the ground floor. My suite was enormous, with three rooms, the size of a flat and beautifully furnished. It was far bigger than the others, I was lucky.

However, about ten meters away was the casino! At first, I wasn't very pleased, "I'll never sleep," I thought. The others came to my door and before I could open it security had pounced. I felt safe after that.

In the casinos, people would play three poker machines all at once. You had to be very careful not to accidentally take 'their' machine. I will play for a little while, but after a short while, I get bored. It was fascinating going behind the scenes, there wasn't a single inch of that casino uncovered by cameras, which was unheard of in other places at that time.

We were taken out to the Hoover Dam. Basically, it's just a big dam. They also took us to an old frontier town, which was utterly deserted, but maintained in good condition. That was fascinating. It looked like the set of a western, with old wooden buildings and places to tie up a horse.

Different hotels invited us to eat there. You could go to any hotel and eat at no cost. At breakfast, the show stars would be there recovering from a night out. I remember seeing Virginia Mayo, who had been Warner Bros biggest star in the 1940s. We had been briefed not to ask for autographs.

We were taken to the Frontier Hotel, which was new. The Frontier included VIP residences, and we were invited to Elizabeth Taylor and Richard Burton's villa. It was very elegant. There was a lot of dark earthy tones, mainly plush red with wooden features. It was simple, with nothing pretentious, but everything was beautifully done. So they wouldn't be bothered, they had 24-hour service to fetch things for them.

It was a lovely trip, and I enjoyed it.

CHAPTER 8: THE STARS

Cary Grant was gorgeous. We were both on the same flight from Los Angeles. It was a rare thing, as most of the luggage had gone and we were both still waiting. It didn't seem to bother him. Cary was quite happy to chatter away.

Marlon Brando. The girl dealing with him went bananas, precisely as we were trained not to. Marlon was very calm about it all, he probably thought she was a nice fan. She wouldn't let anybody else deal with him, so that was a little awkward. She was lucky he was calm, he could have got her sacked.

I also used to book a lot of singers. I can't even remember them all. One night one of the boys dropped coffee over my dress. He was very apologetic and said, "you're not going anywhere special tonight, are you?". Has it happened it didn't stain and dried out fine. However, one of the sales reps piped up, "yes she is, Peggy's off to meet Ella Fitzgerald tonight."

I had indeed been invited to meet Ella Fitzgerald, the top blues singer in the world. She was lovely. I was a little bit in awe. She was a legend.

Another singer I remember is Rod Stewart. I was at the Southern Cross Hotel in Melbourne, which was owned by Pan Am. I went in there and walked up to the lift. Jumping out of the elevator was Rod Stewart and his band. They ran out! He was very apologetic and shouted out "sorry!". Around the back was thousands of teenage girls and he was trying to give them the slip.

Pan Am's Special Handlers at the airports knew how to treat big stars. At that time, they knew how they wanted to be treated, rather like a friend. Some would even leave their cars on our Special Handler's driveway. We're not talking any car, but they knew it would be safe.

Another nice person was Roger Moore. He was at the height of his fame playing James Bond. I can hear him now, "I don't know what I've done to deserve a free ticket, lots more people need it more than I did." I remember saying, "you have done some advertising for us," he replied "oh yeah I did do some, but that seems ages ago," it was just like talking to a friend.

Leonard Nimoy, Mr Spock. He was almost shy. Very nice. A lot of them were quite shy and nervous people.

Not everyone is friendly. Rose Kennedy, President Kennedy's mother, less said, the better. Then there was David Frost, he was so disliked. He always wanted a bulkhead seat in First Class, and nobody was to sit next to him. You can't give a seat away, and I was grateful never to deal with him.

Despite her reputation, Joan Crawford was lovely. She apologised for calling so late. Miss Crawford was just charming, no fuss, no palaver. At that time she basically was the top person in Pepsi, I think she married the man who had owned it. Miss Crawford was travelling for Pepsi, to Atlanta.

CHAPTER 9: THE SOUTH WITH DELTA AIR LINES

My own trip to the south started in Washington DC, with a dress for dinner occasion. I had a very fitting black dress, which had a long scarf, that I put around my neck, with a lovely silver broach.

There were people from Japan, Argentina and all over the world. A glamorous reception in Washington DC, with people from all around the world, felt so exciting.

I spent most of my time with a boy from Argentina and a girl from Japan. I recall we were slightly older than the others.

Our hosts on this trip showed us genuine southern hospitality, chatty, not in a nosy way, but like they were talking to a friend. They'd never be rude, you were their guest to be looked after.

The next morning we flew from Washington DC to Atlanta. That was Delta Air Line's headquarters, and they gave us a behind the scenes tour. At all Delta locations, there was free coffee and danish pastries. Apparently, it started off with people leaving for early flights without time for breakfast. It was very nice.

We were in the maintenance hangers being shown around by Delta's Engineering Director. He showed us a huge ball bearing, a great big thing. I then dropped it on his foot! He was so lovely about it, but I was really embarrassed.

Atlanta was a strange place. Our hotel was brand new, in fact, some areas were still being fitted out. Staying there was the first time I'd been in a lift on the outside of a building. Being modern and tall, you could see for miles. Every time you touched a lift button, there was a static shock!

The next day we moved on from Atlanta to San Francisco. There we rode the cable cars and stayed at the Piedmont Hotel. It was very high, and you looked out over San Francisco. The height was incredible. You could sit there, have your meal, and watch all the lights and cable cars going up and down. It was really nice.

Fishermen's Wharf was pleasant, it was a little bit more than a fishing harbour back then, but not much more. At Fishermen's Wharf, we hunted high and low for a small souvenir that was made in America. Everything was from Japan, and therefore not of much interest to my Japanese friend. The shop keeper told us people weren't interested in the US made souvenirs. She did none the less take us through a curtain to a back room, where there was some American stock.

We then went from San Francisco to New Orleans. The boy who was our guide in New Orleans was fun. He was from New Orleans and taught us you say "New Or-lans" and most certainly not "New Or-lee-Anns"!

We went for a trip down the Mississippi. It's probably me, but I'm not a fan of boat trips, because you see the same thing over and over again. Still, in the afternoon, he showed us around the town.

I can only judge from what I see on the television of today, which horrifies me. There weren't any packed streets or crowds then.

We walked down the streets and then you'd see jazz bands marching around all day. They weren't begging for money, it was just their performance. He took us to some excellent clubs, but let us be honest, they weren't going to take us anywhere seedy.

Our guide lived in the French Quarter and showed us his place before taking us as his guests on a boat at night. He was a musician, and we listened to him play. There was plenty to eat and drink, but nobody was abusive or out of control.

We met the rest of his band. They were mostly older people, and it was like they just jammed with each other. Perhaps they had some preparation, but there was a lot of naturalism about it. Spontaneous jazz, it was lovely. I don't know if people were there all the time, but some in the audience just got up and joined in. I was in my element.

New Orleans is a city with character, unlike a lot of US cities which were new and hadn't developed their own feel just yet. New Orleans had adapted a lot of culture from Africa. Apparently, the slave trade isn't taught about now, which is awful, but I learned about it at school.

I loved the food too, it was spicy. Gumbo was the main dish, a flavoursome food with all sorts of things in it. You always got a plateful.

CHAPTER 10: FROM THE SOUTH TO THE NORTH

Speaking of food, now we move north to Boston. I visited Boston with a colleague who had friends in the area. They booked for us to have a lobster grill. In the end, they couldn't come, so we went. I'd never had lobster. I could eat one right now. The whole thing was an event, a really lovely experience.

We didn't get a chance to see much of Boston. I would have liked to see Harvard, which I believe is very like Cambridge. Visiting in Autumn, they have a lot of red-leaved trees. It really was beautiful. It was also the first time I'd seen Cardinal Birds, which are like ravens but coloured bright red.

My other North American trip was to Vancouver. A friend of mine from Pan Am was Canadian. Her mother came to visit, and I met her. She was a really nice lady and invited me to go and stay. So I did. What I remember the most was taking some Cigars. Without thinking, I took Cuban Cigars. That would be fine, but I transited via the US, where they were banned. I just bought what I thought were nice cigars, as a gift for putting me up for a week. However, customs picked me up! I managed to explain they were for my hosts in Canada. So he let me through, saying "I wish they were mine."

Staying with a family meant I got a good insight into everyday life. In terms of Vancouver, all I remember is a big totem pole. Probably twenty feet high, it represented the traditional culture. We also made a ferry trip over to Victoria Island for lunch.

The family really looked after me.

I made too many training trips to New York to remember. There is, however, one place I want to talk about because it had changed beyond belief. That is Grand Central Station. When I first encountered it, the place was grubby and dirty. I stayed at a hotel at the station. It was the only time I ever stayed in a bad hotel with Pan Am. There were two horrendous incidents, but I won't talk about them. It was old and tatty.

Eventually, New York, with Jacquie Kennedy's help, realised Grand Central is a place to be proud of. It is really quite beautiful. There are so many things that go on there now. I remember my son being there with Mayor Giuliani at a squash tournament. On my most recent visit, I was stunned by the stained glass, which simply wasn't visible before.

In the old days, we were advised not to travel on the Subway without a group. A lot of people were going through good times, but the major cities like New York were feeling massive hardship. With that comes crime. In all the many dozen of visits, never once did I use the subway.

Helicopter from JFK Airport landing on top of
the Pan Am Building early 1960s.

CHAPTER 11: FLYING IN STYLE

One mode of transport I did get to use in New York was a helicopter. I was fortunate that on one of my training courses to New York, I was allowed on the helicopter. Pan Am had a helicopter service from John F Kennedy Airport to the Pan Am Building Roof. Staff were not permitted to travel on it. To this day, I don't know how come I was allowed, it might have been so I could explain it to potential customers.

A Pan Am person escorted you off the plane. We were then driven across directly to the helicopter. I've got no idea what happened to my luggage, but it appeared at the Pan Am Building. I'd never been in a helicopter before. I was lucky and got a seat at the front. The thing that struck me was they left the cockpit door open, which struck me as a bit casual. I was a little nervous when it first took off, going straight up. I'd never done that before. I thought what on earth am I doing this for?

Still, in the end, it was absolutely incredible. When you hit Manhattan, you flew in between the giant buildings. You didn't look down at buildings, you looked up. Landing on the Pan Am roof was strange because going down you can't see. For all, I knew we could have been going down to the street. The pilot thanked us, and there we were, stood on top of the skyscraper roof fifty floors up.

You saw buildings like you don't usually see them. It's hard to explain. I liked looking down because it's a view of New York one never gets. Amongst the buildings, you can't actually see much. Above, it was easy to pick out all the main buildings. After so many visits to New York, I saw the famous buildings without really noticing them. The helicopter was an exception, it was a fantastic experience.

One of my most memorable flights was on American Airlines, just after the 747s came in. The airlines saw it as something special and wanted a signature piece. American Airlines had a cocktail bar with a baby grand piano. You'd sit around and have whatever drink you wanted. It was surreal, something you'd never encountered before. There weren't many places to sit down, but a lot of people enjoyed standing up. The drinks were complimentary, but they were very strict that you couldn't have too many. There was no chance of spending the entire flight hanging around, the idea was every First Class passenger would get a chance. As a concept, it didn't last very long. When times got tough, they converted it to seats.

Pan Am had the Restaurant in the Sky. I was flying back to Australia when I experienced that. The crew asked if I would go up as a representative, "please go because you are part of the company." So I did. At the table was the Chairman of British Paints, the owner of United Travel Agents - an upmarket travel agency, and the CEO of Total Oil. I was hoping there'd be a wife with them to break it up, but no.

We ate and chatted. The Total Oilman had recently flown Concorde. He was a tall man, he said it was great for saving time, but the legroom wasn't any good.

The restaurant had alcoves, with low back seats around dining tables. The cabin crew escorted you upstairs and introduced everyone at the table. They had a restaurant-style menu, and everything was cooked fresh. You were served canapés whilst waiting for the meal to come. It was pleasant, and I ended up enjoying it, I really didn't want to go and make polite conversation, but it turned out well.

Lovely as it was, restaurants don't make money, but selling seats does. So it eventually went away.

747 Restaurant in the Sky publicity
photograph 1970s

At that time, it was still important to travel smartly. I doubt you'd have been let into First Class in jeans or a sweater. I usually travelled in a suit. Casual flying didn't come in straight away with the jumbo, but they caused it.

For me, Pan Am's First Class seats were too big. They were built for men to travel in. To be fair, most first-class passengers were on business and were men. You'd always be served on fine china with anything up to gold cutlery. There wasn't a huge choice of meals, but it was always really nice. For example, if you fancied a fresh omelette, they'd make you one there and then.

The experience was more personalised compared to now. Pan Am would always refer to you by name.

Asian airlines were very much service orientated, they really looked after you. Asian's are family orientated; American's see everyone as the same; then the British are very class conscious. That was shown in the service, airlines reflected their national culture much more then.

I flew British Airways between Australia and the UK a lot. I managed to usually get a single seat by myself, to avoid making small talk. I know I'm biased, but British Airways crews on occasion left a lot to be desired. They were very full of their own importance.

I was once apologised to by an infuriated British Airways captain. The cabin crew's had a staff group going down to Australia. The cabin crew served them before paying passengers. I wasn't in a place to comment, because I hadn't paid. However, the rest had paid full first class fares. The captain was so angry and wanted to talk to me about it. Given a choice, he wanted to send them back home. Despite that, I am very grateful to British Airways in Melbourne for helping me to Europe so much.

CHAPTER 12: VISITING RITA

Someone I was at school with, my friend Rita moved to Paris, which seemed incredibly exciting! She worked with the French Space Agency, sharing a flat on the outskirts of Paris.

Because of my airline career, I was able to go and visit them. I remember they had a grandfather clock with no workings, but if you opened it up, inside had been converted into a drinks cabinet.

We had a lovely time. Rita had a book of walks, and we'd do a different one each time. Rita said we must go and see the Mona Lisa. We just walked straight in, no queues, no entry fee, and we walked right up to the painting.

Paris wasn't very tolerant of visitors. In the restaurants, if you couldn't speak French, they were not going to be nice. Generally, though, people were kind. Where Rita lived, the local shop keepers helped and taught us lots of French. They also explained local customs, like only buying half a loaf, because later on there would be a fresh batch.

In those times there weren't many tourists. Nowadays you see a lot of wealthy looking people in Paris, but not then. I saw ordinary people all the time. Now you go and see designer clothes and marque cars. Then you didn't see that. I think it was more French then Paris was very much a French city. Now it is a world city, with a different feel to the rest of France.

Compared to New York, the food was completely different. It was real French cooking. Portions were small, but it tasted fantastic. French restaurants were almost entirely family-owned. Compared to home, where food was basic meat and two veg, French cooking had different flavours. It was a big step up from what I'd had before, really special.

Unfortunately, Rita had a nasty accident. I don't know the details because she couldn't remember them. Her boyfriend had a little Citroen car, and the accident left her in hospital for a long time. However, no one knew how to get hold of me, so I didn't know about it for a long time.

Coming back from France I got in trouble with customs. I had a dimple bottle of Scotch, which was great for making lamps out of. They told me, "can you get the bottle out," and I went "damn! I wanted the dimple bottle." By mistake, I'd bought the wrong one!

He was confused and when I explained he thought it was funny and waved me on. I never did get a dimple bottle.

Rita came to stay with me and ended up staying a month because of the student riots. There was a curfew, and that meant she couldn't go back. That was enormous fun.

I met up with Rita again who moved to Sydney, just a hop away from Melbourne for me, thanks to my friends at Ansett Airlines. I used to hop up on a Friday night and fly back Monday morning.

Rita's flat was strange. It had one of the best views in Sydney, maybe the world. We'd sit out on the lawn and in front of you was the Sydney Harbour Bridge and Opera House. We used to meet up a lot at weekends and reminisce. We went up to Palm Beach, and all I got was covered in bites! Rita lived at MacMahon's Point. That's a very cosmopolitan area, and we'd visit local craft markets and things like that. You could get everything from earrings to fruit and veg. It was a real local market, with people from lots of places.

Generally, though, Sydney wasn't the international city it is now. Although there were places around the harbour, options for a meal or drink were somewhat limited. Sydney was a very suburban city then. It lacked any real character. Having said that, people were friendly, if you asked for any help they were extremely helpful.

CHAPTER 13: MELBOURNE

Melbourne was probably behind Sydney. On a Sunday today, you could wander out and get a coffee. Then, nothing opened, you couldn't get a coffee, but you could have fired a cannon down Collins St and not hit anything.

At that time, I was living in Jolimont, which was a busy railway junction with goods trains running through the night. It was, however, opposite a lovely park which included Captain Cook's Cottage. My room had a bed which went up into the wall, in theory. It only worked if there was no bedding, so I got used to leaving it down.

The neighbours included members of an opera group and other musicians. Performers don't eat or drink before going on stage, so they'd get back in the evening hungry. When they came back at night, they'd knock on the door with an invitation to join them. They were terrific fun, and I had a lovely time with them.

I also lived for a while in Malvern. I never swore and used to say "fishhooks". The neighbour's girls picked up on that and apparently it took off at school. Their little nephew always had to bring me a flower if he visited, it wouldn't be a little flower, he'd search for a nice big one from somewhere. He was an adorable little boy.

At weekends the Victorian Government Tourist Board used to run weekend trips to places people didn't usually visit. I did weekends away to the Blue Lake, at the time nobody knew why it was blue. Other trips went off to sheep farms to stay for the weekend. On one trip, we even drove through a plague of locust. As you might imagine we were very late arriving and getting into my motel bed what was under the pillow? A locust. I was so tired that I left it there. In the morning, it was still alive, so I put him in my hands and let him out the door.

On another trip, we went to the rainforest, and they showed us the Lyrebird. They build a huge nest, maybe five feet high and are rarely seen.

Melbourne's location is remote. Distance meant many things were a step backwards when compared to other places. People's knowledge of the world wasn't always what it might have been.

I'd often get a call from British Airways or Ansett wanting to double-check their understanding. Pan Am's training at that time was recognised as the best. Ansett as a domestic airline had no reason to know, but as a thank you they looked after me with a supply of free tickets to visit Rita.

One of my friends was engaged to a man who worked in cargo at the airport. He was such a quiet lad, and one day he discovered a package full of smuggled guns. It was Yugoslav terrorists, who were connected to the recent Hilton Hotel bombing in Sydney. The authorities let the guns go to pick up those terrorists when they were delivered.

The airline industry in Melbourne was quite small. I remember one christmas time, lots of staff from the different airlines had become stuck in Hawaii. The problem was so bad, in the end, Qantas sent a 707 to Hawaii exclusively to rescue airline staff, as all the airlines were running out of staff! Being in charge of the Pan Am office in Melbourne at that time, staff being stuck in Hawaii was not an easy explanation to give the big bosses!

With one thing and another, it was time to move on. I was lucky that Pan Am in London said, "that's your desk" and put me to work doing what I'd done for a long time. I was very privileged.

CHAPTER 14: THE FIRST 747

In London, although TWA was supposed to be our great rival, we were very friendly. Mid-morning we'd pop down for a coffee, or they come down to us. That's the way it should be.

Now there is no TWA or Pan Am, and British Airways have retired their last 747s. That seems a bit harsh when you remember it coming in. It was a big occasion. There was nothing remotely like it.

The 747 brought size. There were no budget airlines then, so big planes were the answer to flying more people affordably. Suddenly groups could go on scheduled flights. At that time, there were a lot of family associations. The associations would block book seats and get a better fare. Those cheaper fares meant ordinary people with family who had immigrated could finally visit their long lost relatives.

The 747 was the beginning of cheaper travel. Beforehand, it was expensive to travel. You didn't get too many people travelling for holidays. It was mainly business travel and the odd wealthy person visiting someone.

For staff, there were for's and against's. It was nice for us to work with exited people, off to meet grandchildren they'd never seen. Because people had never been overseas before, they were excited. So from that point of view, it was good.

Before then, if you'd had been in jeans or tatty clothes, you'd probably have been denied boarding. With mass travel, people stopped dressing up, it was the start of dressing to be comfortable.

For airline staff, it made travel more accessible, because there were more seats. It was rare to have a confirmed ticket, so big planes with empty seats were a bonus.

On Waterloo Station in London, before launch, they had a mock-up of the flight deck and some of the cabin. You had to walk up to the actual height, to give you an idea of the size. A lot of people visited because it was something very new.

The inaugural day arrived, but the plane nearly didn't. It was seen off to London by every VIP New York had, with many including congressmen and the mayor. Then an engine failed.

I was in bed, at about six o'clock in the morning the phone went, "Peggy, come in!", of course I said yes. My mission was to catch

VIPs before they left for Heathrow to meet it. A lot of VIPs were heading down to watch it land, and some would then fly to New York.

I jumped in a taxi and when I arrived every senior manager at Pan Am was there. We had the mayor of London, various city types and newspaper people to deal with. Fred Tupper, who was Pan Am's pressman, handled the papers. Fred was a real newspaperman, never messed about, knew everybody in a Fleet St pub and always wore the same Columboesque jacket.

Pan Am at that time knew when to look after people. That morning, we did! In the end, it did eventually arrive. It had been quite a morning.

To my right: Captain Harold Gray (Chairman, Pan American World Airways); Nick Carter (Pan Am LON Chief); my colleague Nick. To my left Vice President Pan Am Atlantic Division

CHAPTER 15: EUROPEAN HOPS

One of the good things about my time working for Pan Am in London was the weekend trips. At that time, I could simply nip away, so I did, and there were too many trips to remember.

Courtesy of Air France, I once had a lunch trip to Nice. We flew First Class, naturally! We literally flew there and back with the plane, but it was a day out and a free lunch.

One other person came with me. It was not a very big plane, with maybe 10 seats in First Class. We were separated, each with a full fare-paying passenger at the side of us.

I sat next to a man called Monty Berman. He owned the major theatrical costumiers for movies and the West End. Monty was very charming, courteous and polite. He always insisted that I was served before him. His travelling companion was one of the major producers, but I didn't catch his name when we were introduced.

We got off in Nice, having chatted all the way. On a plane, I like to be left alone, but this was a pleasant exception. We got off the plane for a coffee, before returning straight back to London.

I did a similar thing to Zurich. Swissair flew us out there. Most of us strolled around the lake, had a coffee and then met up again for a meal. The Swissair representative made sure we had cheese fondue, which was uncommon outside of Switzerland at the time. Zurich was expensive. I think it might have come up at the last minute, which meant that we hadn't plAnnd anything. I wish I had done a bit more studying of maps and things to do. None the less we were well looked after. Recently I used the Swissair hand fan they gave me!

I also went to Athens on two occasions. The first was a weekend trip, again with Margaret. She'd had a strange experience, having had to evacuate via the emergency slides. That had left her badly burnt.

We stayed at Hotel Lybetta. One highlight had to be walking around the Acropolis. I was violently sick up there! Apart from that, we did all the usual sightseeing, as we only really had a day there. I really enjoyed it, exploring the museums and looking around at the pottery shops. The hotel gave us excellent recommendations for food. I can't remember what I had, other than that it was delicious.

On Sunday morning we went down to the harbour. There were a lot of people carrying cases onto the ferries, no backpacks in those days. It wasn't a smart harbour, more like a fishing port. We didn't stay for long because of our flight.

It was a lovely trip, and I enjoyed it.

On another occasion, I met up with my friends Terry and Merrill at her sister's house. Unusually I stayed with them. I don't remember their house, so I'm not sure how we all fitted in. This too was only a weekend trip.

On the first morning, we went out food shopping. First up to the local vegetable market, then onto the fish market for fresh catch. It really was local fishermen directly selling their catch.

These were not tourist places, and local people were pleased to see a visitor. They were very friendly.

With that, we headed down to the beach and barbecued the fish. It was a beautiful small beach, with maybe one other group on it. So very nice.

We also went to a taverna which her sister used a lot. Because they were known, nothing was too much trouble. It was set outdoors, with plants all around it, rather like eating in a garden. Again, it was not where tourists went, this was very much a local spot.

That had been a nice little weekend trip away.

I also made a courtesy trip, I assume with Turkish Airlines, to Istanbul. I'd never been to Istanbul, and it wasn't really on my list of places to go.

I think this trip may have been a full week. We flew out refuelling in Budapest, which was quite interesting. It was my first time in the communist bloc.

In Istanbul, we were met and taken to the hotel.

My friend John Rankmore from Pan Am was there, plus a Lufthansa guy from Frankfurt and two British Airways girls. It was a friendly group, and we blended well together. As the odd one out, I got my own room!

The next day a Turkish Airlines rep came and took us to a souk. There were shops full of gold, absolutely full of it. We looked at the windows, but it was just too much.

Speaking of too much, all of the food was covered in at least a centimetre of oil. It didn't spoil the trip, but we did have to wander around and buy food from little stalls. That included cucumber and little bits of baklava.

We then went to a park, and there wasn't a single woman. Oh dear, we thought, maybe we're not supposed to be here. None the less, we watched some men doing their traditional line dancing. We didn't stay for long as the boys were fine, but us ladies felt uncomfortable.

Our rep then took us to another souk, which had a much more extensive range. There were carpets of course, plus clothes and household things. This was much more what we wanted to see.

One of us bought a carpet, which with haggling took quite a while.

We also visited the old mosque. It was a spectacular building, as is the blue mosque. These were very nice, amongst the loveliest mosques in the world.

Our boat trip on the Bosphorus was spectacular, but it went on for a little bit too long for me.

On the next day, we were taken to a fishing village. Now I believe it is a big holiday destination, but not then. I'm glad I saw it as a fishing village. It was really fun.

The hotel was undergoing a lot of alterations, which meant there was a lot of noise early and late. Unfortunately, that took the edge off it.

We found a disco, which passed the time away and we enjoyed it.

On our last day, back in Istanbul, we went to have dinner at the Hilton Hotel. I couldn't believe it, we got that same meal again, covered in oil! They'd have done whatever we asked, but our mistake was asking for something traditional.

They did, however, serve us a lovely Baked Alaska afterwards!

You didn't see a lot of women in Istanbul, other than some out doing shopping. I had pictures in my mind of the wives being made to stay at home, but that is just my impression and might not be accurate. We certainly did get attention, but nothing that made us uncomfortable.

That's basically Istanbul in a nutshell.

Kuşadası, Turkey

CHAPTER 16: THE MIDDLE EAST

Two girls going on their own to the middle east in the 1960s was odd. I'm embarrassed to say that was probably the appeal. I like to visit before a place becomes popular. When somewhere fills up with tourists, it loses its charm. They begin to cater for generic tourists.

I was very keen to visit Afghanistan. The manager of Ariana, the Afghan airline, was a work friend. He used to come in, collect his mail and drop off some fruit the plane had flown in. Afghanistan wasn't ready for women to visit by themselves. It will be a big fight before Afghan women, and girls get the same as they do overseas. Sometimes there is simply too significant a difference to visit.

I also wanted to visit the northwest frontier. There was already a bit of trouble between India and Pakistan over the Himalayas. As one finds, various countries often claim the same land. Never mind.

I made a weekend trip to Kuwait. That was long before Iraq invaded, so very different times.

There were not many hotels in Kuwait. Generally, the oil companies had their own compounds. I stayed at the Sheraton, and the doorman was a local celebrity. He was very well known and always very welcoming. He was a big man, always smiling and friendly. He was interested to hear what you'd been doing today, whilst still being ultra polite.

On the first day, we were taken out for a short look about, to take some pictures. It was important not to take photos of women. One of our group did, though. There was almost a riot, and it was very scary. People were incredibly up in arms. The representative was local and able to calm things down. There was still huge anger, but the locals accepted it.

Then I saw something hung up in the door of a shop. I thought, "wow, that's lovely. I want that." It was a shop in a tent.

I discovered many years later it is a Bedouin man's wedding coat. Full-length black velvet, embroidered with silk all over. I'd never seen anything like it before, and it was fantastic.

For two hours, the whole group was invited in. We were given padded stools, absolutely everybody came, and the shop attentively kept our coffee cups topped up without fail.

Afterwards, we drove out to an oil well. One of the greatest disappointments of my life! It was only a tiny little pipe, maybe two feet off the ground. That was it. Nothing like you see on television. We never guessed that one day there would be a war over these things.

The Sheraton had a small dance floor and a band, so we all danced the night away. Despite there being coffee pots of whisky everywhere, nobody drunk too much. It was a really happy place.

The oil-rich Kuwaiti's shopped in Paris. I bought various knick-knacks from the stalls were very much for the locals. I thought they were very nice.

The Kuwaitis kept their distance. In the hotel some accompanied western businessmen and they were friendly. However, after the photo incident, we stayed away from most of the Kuwaitis.

We didn't see where Kuwaiti people lived. I don't think we could have gone to a residential area.

Kuwaiti women didn't work. A lot of Egyptian's were employed. I suspect in some places that still applies.

Kuwait from what I understand is now a completely different place, rebuilt after the Gulf War. Back then, it wasn't a big place. The buildings were all white, traditional, designed to keep cool and low in height. Now I gather it is much more modern. I'm glad I saw it when I did. It was a fascinating place to be. You really felt this is somewhere different. Most countries, especially in the cities, are similar. Kuwait was utterly different to anywhere I'd ever been before.

I also went to Beirut, with one of the girls from the office. I'm not sure why we chose Beirut. Probably we could get cheap tickets from Middle Eastern Airlines.

The first thing we did was to buy tickets for the Beirut Casino. In travel, people knew that they put on a spectacular show. I remember a large stage, and there was always something going on. There was singing, dancing and circus-type tricks. We thoroughly enjoyed the evening.

Beirut was the Paris of the east. It was a meeting point of east and west. Perhaps like Dubai today. It is so sad to know what happened.

We stayed at the Mayflower Hotel. There were a lot of English people there. I believe it was extremely popular with Graham

Hill, and one of the Cambridge Spies Kim Philby. He defected to Russia via Beirut.

We saw a day trip to Damascus advertised at our hotel. At the time, there was unrest. However, we thought this is an opportunity we may not get again. So far at least, that has proven right.

So off we went. We then got to the border. Surprisingly the Syrians didn't even ask for our passports. Next thing we knew as the bus drove along, there was nothing but sand. However, there were bumps. Those bumps were tanks, hidden under sand, with guns pointing at us.

I didn't find it frightening. I just never imagined it.

When we got off in Damascus, it was next to a market. All the ladies shopping wanted to talk with us. Amazingly, our tour had two boys from Yemen. They could speak the local language, so translated for us. No one seemed bothered that we didn't have our heads covered. These were ordinary people like us just doing their daily shopping.

I remember one lady, an older lady, telling us how welcome we were in her country. It was lovely. They were all so friendly.

Having been trained not to ask too many questions, we didn't ask a lot. With the political situation, one never knows who is following you. It is easy to get a friendly local person into a lot of trouble.

In the bible, Paul left Israel and wandered off to spread the message. He is supposed to have died under a tree. The tour guide took us to the tree, his explanation was frank, "no one knows, but that's what people say."

The houses were tiny, made of brick and plaster. There were no pavements, apart from at the market. Otherwise, it was just regular dirt.

Via the two boys, we were chatting to some people. One of the men then came running out. He had a little brass dish, which I have in my lounge to this day.

I fell in love with Syria that day. I still want to go back, but I suspect it is off the cards. It was the people they were just so friendly, so lovely. I get horribly upset at what has happened. Those people have been through so much now.

CHAPTER 17: AFRICA

We decided to go a couple of days before our tour of South Africa started. I can't say I liked South Africa, apartheid was a nasty thing. However, I'll explain why this was my favourite trip later on.

Sabena then took us out to Kruger National Park. We stayed in typical little round safari huts. We were so excited to see some Impala, plus some wildebeest. The elephants didn't like us, one of them lined up to charge us. My money was on him winning. I can't remember lions, but I suppose we must have seen some.

We then headed up to Pretoria, the Capital. That was where I saw jacaranda trees in full bloom.

We had a day trip to one of the tribes, but not to any townships. The white South African's told us not to wear any jewellery or watches or bags because the tribe would steal them. We were also told not to enter their craft huts. I, of course, did and bought some little beads. It was clear the whites were making sure we left believing the blacks were backward and untrustworthy.

All the people I knew who spent any sort of time in South Africa left as quick as they could. Apartheid expected you to treat people dreadfully.

They say sometimes it's the journey and not the destination that counts. My trip to Africa is one such case.

We got to Brussels no problem. Sabena, who are no longer with us, was not fun. There were lots of babies hung up from hammocks. I sat there, expecting them to fall down at any minute.

The plane stopped in Madrid, and there we were offloaded. Not only that, but there were also no onward flights. All I remember of Madrid is one enormous square. I've got no idea what it was or where it was.

Our hotel was extremely basic. My room had a bed and a multicolour bedspread, that's all, but the staff were friendly though.

So, back to Brussels. With a day to ourselves, we went into Central Brussels, but I can't remember much about that. Our replacement flight would only go as far as Kinshasa. However, that was a step nearer, so we did it.

When we landed, there was almost no English spoken. The locals spoke a form of French. Luckily, there had been a lot of missionaries on the flight, and they were very kind, translating for us. Without them, we'd never have got through.

There was a Pan Am office in Kinshasa, and they found us somewhere safe to stay. The Pan Am staff told us in no uncertain terms that we had to keep to the main street.

The police were dressed like those in Paris. At a huge junction, with four multi-lane streets, there was a policeman directing traffic. He was really keeping things organised. But he wanted a picture, so he stopped four dual-carriageway streets of heavy traffic until we had finished taking our photos of him!

We also visited a market. The week before there had been a public hanging. So they'd had to move the market. Although the civil war was officially over, there was still much bloodshed.

For dinner, we went to a little cafe, because the hotel no longer had a restaurant. The building was lovely, one wall of my room was stunning carved wood, but the plumbing didn't work. Nothing worked. The civil war had caused a lot of destruction.

We made it back to the Pan Am office. One of the boys said, "we've been waiting for you". He took us down a side road of little houses, saying, "they know you're coming". The street was tranquil, with small homes on their own plots of land. They were one step up from a hut. It looked as if the road had been hardened and flattened, but not tarmaced.

Walking along, we could see people outside waiting. I've no idea who the people were, other than that they were all local. They were very excited. We went into their very tiny little backyard. There was the most enormous crocodile I've ever seen before or since. It had been caught out of the Congo river a few days earlier. The river was an important water source for them.

The crocodile was in perfect condition, and they were feeding him. That was quite exciting!

After seeing him, I've never really felt any other crocodile was massive. All the other ones I've seen have been babies compared to him. He was amazing. I can't stress how big he was.

The locals were really excited that we were there. We might as well have been aliens in The Congo.

To give an idea of how bad things were, the Sabena check-in staff at the airport were begging for money from us.

Then, lots of mercenaries appeared. Their sergeant came to sit with us, to stop the others pestering us. White girls simply didn't exist.

Two young mercenaries didn't want to go back. They'd been sent home once before, but then disappeared before their flight. So this time the officers were there to make sure they'd got on the plane.

Some of the mercenaries came up to say they'd seen us on the same street.

President Mobutu then landed in slight rain. I remember a 60 Minutes Programme in Australia, when Richard Carlton hit someone, well that was Mobutu. The president wouldn't get off his plane due to the rain, and the airport remained closed.

The stewardesses were pleased to see us. They warned it was common for the mercenaries to get drunk and shoot at each other.

We sat with a senior mercenary officer, but he was being sent home as his nerves were broken. Much of their fighting was against child soldiers. He didn't know that he wasn't coming back. However, being a senior, it meant the others didn't pester us.

He was fascinating because he knew the whole of Africa like the back of his hand. He'd tell us about sites to look out for. It was fascinating.

On his blazer, he had a badge. It looked a bit bulky. He kept touching it. I'm sure it was hiding diamonds.

One of the other mercenaries was smuggling a parrot. Because of the delay, the parrot woke up long before landing. When we did land, the South African Police were waiting to arrest some of them.

Rather sadly, our flight back was very uneventful!

CHAPTER 18: MY RETURN TO NEW YORK

I like Facebook. Back in 2010, a Facebook campaign to "Save the Pan Am Worldport" launched. The Worldport was Pan Am's original terminal at New York's Kennedy Airport. It resembled a giant UFO. America doesn't have a lot of history, and the Worldport represented a time when America led the world. A place of the jet-set from the space age.

Reading updates on my i-pad brought back many memories of New York, which I'd not visited for decades. Sadly, the campaign failed, and the terminal was torn down. Still, the giant skyscraper Pan Am Building in central Manhattan stands. I was determined to visit it one more time.

With all my travel concessions long gone, that was simply impossible. So I knew it would probably never happen. Such is life.

Then in 2015, my son John-James quit his job and had a month off before starting a new one. When he offered to take me, I had a lot of worries about it.

I managed to pack everything into one small shoulder bag. That's a skill I learned late in travel. Sat on the airport coach with my bag beside me, I could have watched the endless motorway. But I sat concerned. Will I be embarrassed about pacemaker security searches? I've got my glasses off and hair swept back in my passport, it looks nothing like me! I know that sounds stupid, but my passport photo looks nothing like me. With the rudeness and queues at US immigration, I wasn't looking forward to it.

I have always worried before flights. Check-in is when I relax. Of course, you don't check in anymore. So it wasn't until the lounge that I could start to enjoy things. Lounges were not so common when I worked for the airlines. Fewer people travelling, meant there was very little need for them.

Today they are a lovely place to relax in a big comfortable seat with a coffee and have some breakfast.

Another improvement compared to the original long-haul jets, is seating. The modern long-haul jets often have blocks of just two seats. I was really pleased about not sitting in the middle of three.

I don't know why, but it felt like I hadn't made a long trip before. Looking back, I was worried about US immigration. However, I have to be nice about Delta Air Lines. The crew was very personable, and we always got served first. After all of my concerns, we walked straight up to US immigration, and the young officer couldn't have been more welcoming.

My next pleasant surprise was the taxi queue. Gone was yesteryear's chaotic crowds. We walked straight up to an orderly queue, paid the set fare and off it was to Midtown Manhattan.

I couldn't get used to how New York had changed. On my first visit, most pavements were reasonably empty. So you could see far along the dead straight avenues and look up at huge skyscrapers. Now the vista is entirely hidden by crowds, and hoards will knock over anybody looking up.

My next big surprise was j-walkers. J-walking used to be an easy catch for the New York Police. You'd be made to walk around a junction in circles using the pedestrian lights if they caught you. Nobody J-walked in New York then, now everybody is at it!

Another shock was safety. Colleagues on my New York trips were mugged, stabbed, and even raped. We were advised not to venture outside of midtown Manhattan, not to take the subways under any circumstances, and not to walk out anywhere after six in the evening.

It was a shock to me that New York felt safe. After checking in to the hotel, I went for a wander by myself. At the street corner, there was what looked to be a subway entrance, so I walked in. I was after some snacks for the room and found a small pharmacy. Then I came across a little cafe for coffee. Sure the building needed some refurbishment, but the police with guns made me feel safe. It turned out I was in the Port Authority Bus Terminal, not New York's most glamorous location, but it was safe to venture there.

Sometimes glamorous locations don't turn out to be all that nice. Times Square was a little disappointing. It was nice being sat at a cafe table watching the news tickers. But the pavements are full of poorly fitting character outfits you pay to have a photo with. It's rather sad.

Wandering around New York, there is always something going on. Take Stars in the Alley. The two-hour free concert celebrates the end of the Broadway season. There was a large bill of Broadway stars from Chicago, Wicked, Matilda, The Lion King, and Kinky Boots, to name but a few. It was lovely to watch such talented top performers. I've still got the free water bottle they gave me!

That morning Stars in the Alley host Darren Criss walked past as I had breakfast. Every morning I sat at tables outside for breakfast in the sun on the sidewalk. With hedges to block out traffic, it was the best way to have breakfast in New York on a sunny day.

On my many flights between the West Coast and Australia, hot pastrami rolls were served as a snack. They were delicious. The home of Pastrami in New York is Katz's Deli. It broke my heart! My plate had piles of beautiful pastrami, much too much for me! In America, you can take leftovers home in a doggy bag, but I didn't fancy carrying one around all day.

My favourite place to eat was quite simple but very friendly. It was an old-style New York Cafe in Hells Kitchen. There used to be lots of similar cafes, especially around Lexington Avenue, but they had all gone. The first time I ate at my Hells Kitchen favourite, our waiter said, "it's only my first day." Having heard that one before, I didn't take it too seriously but based upon his hesitance, it really was. I loved the Quesadilla, which was new to me; I couldn't even say it. Every time I went back, the staff welcomed me like an old friend, escorting me to 'my' table. It was so lovely to be welcomed and have a friendly conversation.

I found it easy to talk with people in New York. Catching a cab back on Saturday afternoon, I struck up a conversation with a taxi driver from Senegal. You don't get a chance to do that every day in ordinary life.

Another conversation I vividly remember was at the September 11 Museum. The museum is in a giant underground space. Artefacts include wrecked emergency vehicles, including a crushed fire engine and pieces of metal from all seven World Trade Center buildings. There are pictures of the victims, plus wreckage, and general destruction. Inside smaller rooms, there are recordings of victims, phone calls from the hijacked aircraft, and 911 phone calls. Entombed are the unidentified remains of 1,115 victims. It all became a little bit too much, so I went for a coffee upstairs.

Upstairs a young lady volunteer came over to talk. She would have been roughly my age when I first visited more than five decades before. All of the volunteers lost someone during 9/11. She started with small talk asking where we were visiting from. When I told her the reason for my visit, she couldn't believe it.

She spent the next twenty minutes asking questions about her city, from me, a tourist!

It isn't easy to convey just how life in New York felt around the 1960s and 70s. Signs everywhere warned you to mind your valuables and to keep jewellery tucked away. Worst was the idea that anything could happen, anywhere, at any time. You became alert and always had your handbag around the front. A lot has improved, and I did my best to emphasise these things for her.

Grand Central Station is a great example. It used to be filthy, left in such disrepair some parts were in serious danger of collapse. Seeing the beautiful windows restored, shiny marble, charming shops, and places to eat were fantastic. I loved it and could have spent a holiday there.

On top of Grand Central is a giant skyscraper with "MetLife" emblazoned across the top. That broke my heart; it will always be the Pan Am Building.

I'd made it. I was back in the giant stone walled lobby, where once I'd caught my first express lift, direct to the 44th floor. I remembered my first Caesar Salad, from the canteen once above. It was strange being back, with all the sales offices and promotions gone. There is, however, a lovely sculpture dedicated to Juan Trippe and Pan Am's staff, which at least commemorates we were once there.

I'd done it, but there was no reason to hang around.

Being invited to One World Trade Center's opening ceremony was fantastic. There had been a celebrity event the night before, but being at the ribbon-cutting for such a historic event was terrific.

It was unseasonably, warm and sunny. The enormous tower stood and shone, reflecting cloudless blue skies. Gauging its height is nearly impossible. There must have been a few hundred people, but we were right at the front surrounded by the press. It was a simple but uplifting ceremony. Young school-age Broadway performers, stars of tomorrow, performed musical acts. I got talking to a nice lady on my left. She had been a school bus driver for years and had brought the performers. She told me about the kids and their performances. It was a lovely personal insight.

Inside, you look down. I can't quite describe how you have to peer at tiny buildings way below, which shockingly are huge skyscrapers themselves. It's like being in a helicopter.

The beautiful blue sky held out until we grabbed a taxi to Kennedy Airport. On the Queensboro Bridge, a colossal thunderstorm erupted. That, unfortunately, shut the airport, but it didn't matter - this had been a wonderful trip.

My return to Grand Central Station, New York

Ribbon Cutting Ceremony, the new One World Trade Center

CHAPTER 19: UKRAINE

My first memory of Kyiv was getting out of the airport. There was no fuss or bother. It was one of the very few times I've looked for someone with a board with my name on it. A very smart looking military-style gentleman escorted us to his awaiting Mercedes. He wasn't very talkative.

It was a long drive-in. All I knew is we were staying on a boat. I wasn't prepared for a splendid river cruise style vessel. It had lovely big balconies, and the room was absolutely gorgeous.

There was a beautiful iron-framed bed, everything was spotlessly tidy with a sofa and table set on the balcony. The balcony was riverside, and I could spent a week just sat there enjoying the boats and ships going past.

The restaurant wasn't open, so it was room service. I seem to remember my son having Filet Steak every day, it was delicious and extremely cheap. With my river bass and a bottle of wine, it was delightful.

There were all sorts of boats, from kaiaks to hydrofoils. You could see a giant war memorial statue in the distance, which was absolutely massive.

The next morning we went to an ancient monastery. There were lots of people everywhere. It is really a compound of monasteries. We didn't go in all of them as it would have taken too long. The buildings were beautifully kept. Inside the tiling, in a sort of wedgwood blue colour, was hard to believe. All topped off by gold onion dome tops.

Next up was a local Marshrutka. That's a kind of minibus, and it's very unusual. You cram on, maybe getting a seat. Luckily we did. To pay, you hand your money to the passenger in front, who in turn gives it to the person in front, until it eventually reaches the driver. Any change then comes back to you the same way.

The local market was fantastic. It was my first time seeing tiny little shops, basically like a kiosk. They were absolutely everywhere, dozens and dozens in just a single underpass. It was great to think that they all supported a family.

Fro the main market, my most vivid memory is of new potatoes. An older man was selling them, and it looked like everything had come out of his allotment. There were lots of little stalls, books, second-hand clothes, toys, you could probably buy just about anything. I especially remember the jams and preserves. It was a real proper market.

Next stop was a brand new mall, and to get in one had to pass an airport-style security check. That was a culture shock. There were many international brands in there, but it gave us somewhere to eat, and the food was traditional.

We then got the Metro into central Kiev. People always stood up to give me a seat. You don't hear that sort of thing about Ukraine.

Kyiv's main street was very different from the rest of the city. We'd seen lots of small streets, but this was an enormous wide boulevard. The style was very Soviet. For most of my life, Kyiv was the third Soviet city. There has been a lot of civil unrest before my trip and signs were still around. Kyiv's main square was still partly boarded up and you could see bullet holes on some of the buildings.

Just next to our boat was a little beach, which gave a beautiful place nearby to stroll around. There was a little family-run hut by the river, they were so pleased to have foreigners stop. It might seem strange, but they were happy we stopped and sat down. Most people just grabbed a bottle of water and went. The fact we sat down really seemed to make them happy.

Another friendly little cafe was at the main train station. My son went off to a museum nearby, and I found a small cafe for coffee and a pastry. The lady was very talkative, she didn't work full time and had to be home for the children from school. She'd been there a long time, people were friendly, quite liked it. She was pleased to practice her English.

Next up was a Sunday market with all sorts of brick-a-brak, plus bands playing. I could have got carried away buying things. It was such a friendly and relaxed place. Unfortunately, the paving was very uneven, and I fell over, that's bifocal glasses for you. The Ukrainian's around were so lovely. People flocked to help, they brought blankets out, and older lady wouldn't leave until I got up.

It wasn't just the older generation either. Some younger girls wanted to talk about Pippa Middleton's wedding and her dress.

Ukraine was less Russian than I imagined it would be. The people were very friendly. Your form views of countries, but you have to visit to find out what they're really like.

Kyiv Metro, people always stood to give me
a seat

Gun shot damage from recent civil unrest in Kyiv's main square

A local market in Kyiv, you could have bought anything here

The view from my balcony, with John-James.

CHAPTER 20: ICELAND

I'd just come out of almost four months of COVID isolation. For that whole time, because of my age, I couldn't have contact with anybody except at a distance. So it was nice to visit somewhere which, at that time, had a fairly normal lifestyle.

Iceland isn't a place I was ever interested in. There didn't seem to be much by the way of older buildings and it is mostly country. I'm more a city girl, but what an eye opener this trip was.

Considering these pandemic times, Holiday Inn was very well organised. I was pleasantly surprised they still offered food if you wanted it and that breakfast available at 4am.

I suspect because I had no idea where I was going, the short walk to the terminal seemed very long.

Being my first flight since the pandemic began, I didn't know what to expect. I thought easyJet was very good. We had to wear our face masks all the time, except when we were eating and drinking. I was impressed that despite COVID, everything was highly organised and the cabin crew were extremely professional, reassuring and organised.

Landing at Keflavik I had to be tested for COVID-19, as does everybody arriving. I'd not been tested before. Thankfully there were people directing everyone along, checking the QR barcode on your phone at each point.

Instead of the usual passport line, there was a long row of portable cubicles. Thankfully there was no queue, with just one family in front of me. Someone kind of stood outside and signalled me in. I didn't know what to expect.

It was fairly simple, you show a barcode and passport to prove you're not someone else. They then took a throat swab which wasn't too bad, however I didn't like the nose swab, but thankfully it was over quickly. Test done they gave me a leaflet and a passport officer explained how you get your result via text message.

Despite these border formalities being new, it was all so easy. The results came though in a couple of hours too.

A nice part of the trip was being chauffeured around by my son, who picked me up in a nice four wheel drive. Being early we headed for a coffee shop in Keflavik, where I had the best cinnamon roll I'd had in years.

I was surprised Keflavik is quite far from Reykjavik, but a very pretty drive.

My son then took me for a lobster lunch. It was beautiful, a curry soup with chunks of lobster, right up my street. I could do with a bowl tonight! The cafe was very retro, with old style furniture, all be it in nice condition.

From there we went back through an enormous long tunnel to Reykjavik itself and an extremely nice flat. Along the way we'd stopped to buy some food at a local supermarket, but my first attempt at traditional Iceland food wasn't a success, it tasted awful!

The next day we went out early for a drive. First up we had breakfast at the docks. It was very interesting to see fishing boats and the processing factories.

We then went to the Reykjanes Peninsula, which is a UNESCO Global Geopark. Here the ground is black, all volcanic, there are no animals and the only foliage is moss. It's very lunar, in fact the first astronauts practiced here.

Once you get off the main routes, the roads are not necessarily tarmac, so I was glad we had a four wheel drive. I'd never been in a four wheel drive other than in a city, so this was a brand new experience.

We passed over the tectonic plate between Europe and North America. Having crossed between the two many dozens of times, I'd never thought about where the two begin and end.

We also visited some stunning cliffs and the sulfur flats. In the distance there were contrasting ice capped mountains.

Afterwards we stopped a volcanic lava cave, which made me a bit worried as I had visions of them collapsing in. It was truly stunning though.

The next day we visited a local market. It was what I call a proper market, where you could buy ornaments, clothes and food from ordinary local traders.

I also fed some horses at a museum with old buildings saved from demolition. Feeding the horses took me back to my young days. They were lovely natured little horses, it was really fun.

That day we also had a very nice meal at a Michelin Starred restaurant.

The Icelandic geysers were amazing, I don't even have words to describe them. I was so excited to see one of the little geysers erupt, as apparently they tend to rest most of the time.

I became truly fascinated by the landscape. Obviously not everything is volcanic, but to have that amount of lava rock, throughout history there must have been some vast eruptions.

I got a little scared by some of the mountain roads, I didn't like a big bang as we reversed because of a river that was flooding the road. However, the views are stunning.

The scenery is beautiful, it's really everywhere, not just in little pockets. Just looking at country is boring to me. Yet because the landscape is so unusual, that didn't happen.

As you've read in this book, I've been to a few places. Yet Iceland is very different to anywhere else I've visited in the world. To my amazement, I absolutely fell in love and was sad leave. Despite the pandemic, this was one of the best trips I've ever had.

Printed in Great Britain
by Amazon